Roommates

To

Romance!

12 Minutes a Day to Passion

Corkie Mann

Best Selling Author

*You are About to
Experience the
Most Beautiful
Love Story
Ever Told …*

Yours

Contact Information for:
Couples Mentoring
Marriage Retreats
Professional Key Note Speaker

Corkie@CorkieMann.com
CorkieMann.com
Social Media:
@CorkieMann

Dedicated to:

My Loving
Sweetheart Dennis

*This is an unusual
book,
It's to*
**Soften your heart
and fall in love much
deeper and richer than
you've ever imagined.
Read it alone or
together daily, then
soon you can read just
the bold print much
faster.**

*Imagine Your
Spouse has a
"Bucket"
That you fill with
Love,
Understanding,
Support,
Kindness,
Happiness, and
Respect
each day.*

Take a look right now at their "Imaginary Bucket".

Is it Filled to Overflowing?

*Is it Half Full?
Or is it Completely Dry?*

*For the **next** 90 days* read each page of this book and

give it your all! 100%...

Will you commit to giving your Spouse 100%? Say Yes! and let's get started.

*Give to them,
and then Give
with all your
Heart, and
then Give
some More.*

Fill their Bucket so that it Overflows Every Day.

*To have a
Mighty
Change,*

*You must
first change
Yourself.*

"God grant me the ***Serenity*** to accept the people I cannot "change", the ***Courage*** to "change" the one I can, and the ***Wisdom*** to know.....
*it's **Me!**"*

John H. Miller

They say that marriage is "hard work". This is what they mean….

The Hard Work is Letting go of Selfishness.

Your Marriage Commitment

Your Wedding Vows went something Like… Do you <u>Promise</u> to <u>Love</u>, <u>Honor</u> and <u>Cherish</u>, <u>Right?</u>…...

LOVE…. Is Unconditional
HONOR…. Is Respect
CHERISH… Is to Adore,
Through…
Good times and Bad,
Sickness and Health,
Rich or Poor.

Let go of Yourself, And... Just Love

These Vows are
promises And
they aren't
always that easy
to follow…
But they are the
answer to a
Wonderful
Marriage.

Love ,
Honor,
& Cherish.
To truly Love in
Marriage, you
must have
Unconditional
Love.

Making one
another
wrong,
belittling,
Selfishness
is not Love.

Do Nice
Things for
each other,
*Encourage
and Uplift.*

Be Nice

Do Something Nice for Your Honey Today

Say Nice Things. Or say Nothing at All…

Just Smile if that's all you have, and BE NICE.

Smile!
With Love

Top of the list of what People want is Love and Attention

Just an "I Love You Smile" Will Move Mountains

*Support
Each Other*
We All have
Differences of
Opinions,
Likes, &
Dislikes.

Honor One another's Ideas as Long as They're Moral, Legal, and Ethical

"I Love You"

**Tell each other
every day,**
more than once a day.
Everyone loves to hear
"I Love You", and
We also love to hear
**"You are So Wonderful"
Bottom line talk
lovingly & Kind to
One Another**

Admire Each other

Tell them What You Admire about them. While you are telling them how wonderful they are, tell them why, and what it is they do that's so Wonderful.

Have you ever noticed how women like to read romance novels, and watch romantic movies?

Men, Pay attention! Most Women, love to be Romanced!

Most of the
time, it's the
*Little things
that make a
huge
difference!*

If you don't know what they Want…*ASK!*

This is Valuable Information!

Ladies, Pay attention! Sometimes just ***Lovingly slip your arm through his*** and hold his strong arm, like he's escorting you. He'll feel like he's your protector.

Find time to have Romance in Your Marriage, Today!

Men, Romance
may not be what
you think it
is…It's treating
her with love,
thoughtfulness,
and kindness.
Watch the Chic
Flicks with her
and those movies
just might teach
you, *ASK!*

Sway

Stand up and Hold each
other
Now sway back and
forth to your favorite
slow song.
Take 2 minutes a day,
Ohh what a difference it
will make!

**No Talking
Just Lovingly
Smile.**

Snuggle

Find the time to just hold one another.

Trust the Intention of Each other's Heart

Trust is so Essential in Marriage.

They didn't
wake up today
and try to figure
out just how to
make you feel
miserable, look
and see, or ask
where their heart
is, and what they
need from you.

*Most hurts
are from
Misunderstandings*

Talk,

Listen, with an open
heart and
Understanding heart.
Then if you're still
hurt
Ask yourself…
Is this really going to
matter 10 years from
now? ….No?
Then let it go.

***If you are
Truly Hurt***
and need some
clarification
Then sit down
together and have a
heart to heart talk.
Explain what is
going on, and how it
is affecting you and
your relationship.

STOP!
Bringing up stuff
from the past
The only way
you can have a
better Future is
to give up all
hope for a
better Past.

Just Let it go! There's always going to be things that went wrong, that hurt, that may have even torn you apart. Leave it alone. Take each other by the hand and go forward together.

This isn't always that easy, but eventually it will bring joy to your lives.

Give All Your Heart

Let go, and you'll find that giving all your heart is the best way for your sweetheart to receive All of You.

Open yourself to passionate love.

Are you Ready for Passionate Love?

Passion!!!

When You First knew you were in love, there was Passion right?

These are
Feelings
*You Can
Recreate,*
and They are the
Fuel to the Fire
to Create
Happiness in
Your
Relationship.

Those Feelings Were Once There, and *You Can Find Those Feelings Again!*

*If the
Passion
spark isn't
there quite
yet...*

*Every day
close your eyes
for about 30
seconds and
see yourself
snuggling,
smiling.*

Feeling all those "wonderful" feelings of how you want to feel in your Relationship.

*See your
Marriage
Harmonious
and Happy
in your
mind...*

*What you see
think and feel
in your mind
is what you
are creating
for tomorrow.*

Flirt

Wink, Smile, Play, and Just Plain Have Fun.

**Find Time
for each other
Nothing's more
important than
receiving
attention.**
*The Truth is,
You'll Find time
for the Things
That are
Important.*

*Put Each
Other
High on the
Priority List
Every day.*

Your Time is the most Valuable Gift You can Give in Your Relationship!

Dance in
the
Kitchen

Find Out What
Is
Romantic
to your Honey
Hold each
other,
Smile, Play
Take the time
Every Day.

Put each other on a pedestal

When you're both on the Pedestal…your Relationship is in a Phenomenal place.

Discover what they like, and what makes them feel Special.

What does Your Honey like to do, what movies, favorite restaurant, & gifts.

She wants you to "just know" what she wants and likes. Find out & lovingly surprise her.

Be Grateful

Daily, Tell them that You Appreciate them. Seek to find something nice to say daily, especially "Thank You".

Kiss

Kiss often, and not just a little peck. Find 10 seconds in your day, and kiss, yes kiss for 10 seconds. You remember…

Chivalry...

Many couples today have lost this fine art in their relationship. He opens the door and allows his lady to go first. She feels special. Let her order her meal first, offer your coat. Men are meant to be the protectors, and it makes them feel good

Ladies allow him to be your Knight and Shinning Armor. "Knight in Shining Armor"

Laugh

Play, Find Funny
Movies,
Homemade
Sports, Picnics.
Find Fun Stuff to
Do Together that
You Both Enjoy.

Lighten up and play.

*Find the
Good
In each other*

Make a list
of all the things you
Love and Admire
about them.
Even if you need to
go back in time and
find the things that
attracted you to one
another.

Be Open and Honest

Lovingly Tell the Truth, Be Open, with how you feel, your Likes and Dislikes. Always use tact.

Integrity

Do what you say you'll do, for yourself and to others.

Have concern
for each other, if
you're thinking
of saying
something, Stop!
First ask
yourself could
this hurt their
feelings. Use
good judgement.

Be Considerate

Put your
sweetheart first
with no
expectations and
Then watch and
see how fast your
love grows.

Keep Others Opinions Out of Your Relationship

Don't share with others…Your "Dirty Laundry" It just adds fuel to the raging fire. Keep it to yourself, because it's so very hurtful.

Never Tolerate Abuse or Violence

Abuse and Violence
is just plain
Not allowed,
Physically, or
Mentally.
Abuse is not Love.
You do not deserve
it, no matter what
you do, you never
deserve abuse! …..
Stop making
excuses, and get
help!

Abuse is just plain wrong! Get Professional Help Right Now, <u>Today!</u>

You & your children will be scarred forever, don't allow abuse to continue for another minute.

*Have you ever noticed
how ornery men get
when it's that time of
the month for her?*

*AND they can't seem
to do anything right,
and no matter what
She does, He always
wants to start a fight?
Okay, a bit sarcastic,
but that's how she
sees it.*

That "Crazy time of
the Month". Even
though she thinks
she's totally normal,
most of your "fights"
will happen during
this time. Be extra
sensitive to her
feelings, be loving
and kind, and just stay
out of her way. Let
her be right. She'll be
okay in a few days.

It's best to keep track of
her monthly schedule,
Ask when her cycle is.
Have it on a calendar,
This way you are
"prepared" for the
craziness.
Also, Never mention
that she's crazy during
this time,
It'll make it worse.

***Men* have a hard time figuring her out, don't even try to…**
Sometimes she can't even figure herself out. Guys, when she "blindsides you" just try and stay out of her way, don't take offence, she'll be alright in a few days. Later on in the month, nonchalantly, ask her when her cycle is "even though she's normal during that time" This way you can be a bit prepared for the storms.

***Stop making
Your Honey
Wrong, be
tactful and
loving when
you're honest,
and take
responsibility for
your opinion.***

*In Case You
Haven't
Noticed… We're
a Bit Different
From One
Another.*
*The Next 2 Pages
Should Be a Big Help
Understanding Our
Differences.
It was described
perfectly in a talk by
Mark Gungor…*

A Man's brain

has many little boxes in them, and only one box is allowed open at a time. He may have a box open, say "The Football Box" and if his wife tries to talk to him, he has to put that box away, and find "The Wife Box" to hear what she has to say. But, if he's watching a football game, he probably won't want to put that box away, and take out her box. He knows he can't do both, right? Men, it might be a good idea to talk to her before the game and explain this to her, or plan on "pausing" the TV when she wants to talk.

Women have a hard time understanding this because

<u>*Woman's brains*</u>

can do several things all at the same time without a hic-up. Men are great at doing one thing at a time, while Women can cook dinner, talk on the phone, and match color swatches for designing her "new Kitchen" all at the same time. Women's brains are wired a bit differently, instead of boxes they have something that looks like

Swirling Spaghetti

Men are Usually Oblivious to Women's Needs.
*So, Men, if you want to know what she wants, or what she's thinking…
It's simple!*
Ask Her. *… and find out.
What's Her favorite date?
Favorite Flower? Perfume?
This is the*
"Data Gathering" *time.*
Then…Surprise her. *She just wants you to think of these things yourself, and spontaneously do them…*
That's Romantic.

Ladies this is too easy,
***When Men say
something….
Listen to Him***
You may try to make it
much more complicated.
You may say to yourself
"He doesn't mean that"
and then you'll come up
with your own version
of HIS story.
Stop it!
Listen to Him

Sometimes men feel the need to Go to his "Cave"

This is usually what Guys do.
They shut down in order to
re-program.
That way he can resolve it
in his mind.
Men, make sure she knows
this, and that you are
processing the situation.
Explain to her that this is the
way you resolve these matters,
and that you will be back to
talk.
***Agree on a time to calmly
talk about it.***

Ladies, have you ever noticed that you can read other women's minds? You just know what they mean without them finishing what they are saying? Ok, well men can't do this. Most men can't read your mind, Ever, so don't expect it.
And in that same light, you think you can read His mind, You may actually put words in His mouth. The Truth is, you haven't a clue as to what he's thinking,

Let Him Tell you what he's thinking.
You want Him to Talk to You, then listen to Him

Talk

When you say anything, come from how **YOU feel**, no dumping.

*Remember
no one can
make <u>You</u>
feel a
certain way,
Only You
Can.*

When someone has been made wrong, they probably won't risk being made wrong again.

Appreciate

each other and tell them what appreciate about them, and all they do for you.

Be Nice

Give constructive suggestions. So, if he puts the baby's diaper on backwards, let it be. If she forgets the cream in your coffee, let it be okay, or talk about it and laugh. You don't need to fault find.

When
friction
starts to
come
between you
two…
Join forces

Stick Together
Remove the
"Problem" from
"Between You
two" and move it
...out away you
both. Now,
conquer the issue
together. You now
have two loving
people, against one
Problem.

Think of
nice things
to do for
one another.

Even Just a
loving

Smile

Might be all that
you need.

Have a
Date Night
Once a
Week

Your Dates take top priority over everything. Together decide on your Dates. Mark it on your calendar for once a week.

*What
Do you each
Like to Do?*

This week set aside some time to plan with the kids in bed, TV off, and especially have eye contact.

***Make a list of
all the things***
you two would
enjoy doing
together. And
agree to do
somethings just
because you want
to enjoy being
together.

Be Sensitive to each other's Ideas.

Hold Hands Often

Don't wait, just reach out and hold their hand.
Sit and snuggle…Or better yet, make time in the mornings to snuggle.

*Courting
is a
Lifetime
Experience.*

Make Love
Often

You can take her out of this World. Talk to Her, Ask her what she likes and what you can do. **Women usually take longer than men,** *so be patient with her. This is why women fake it. They feel they are taking too long.*

Disclaimer:
This may create babies

How to turn on a man

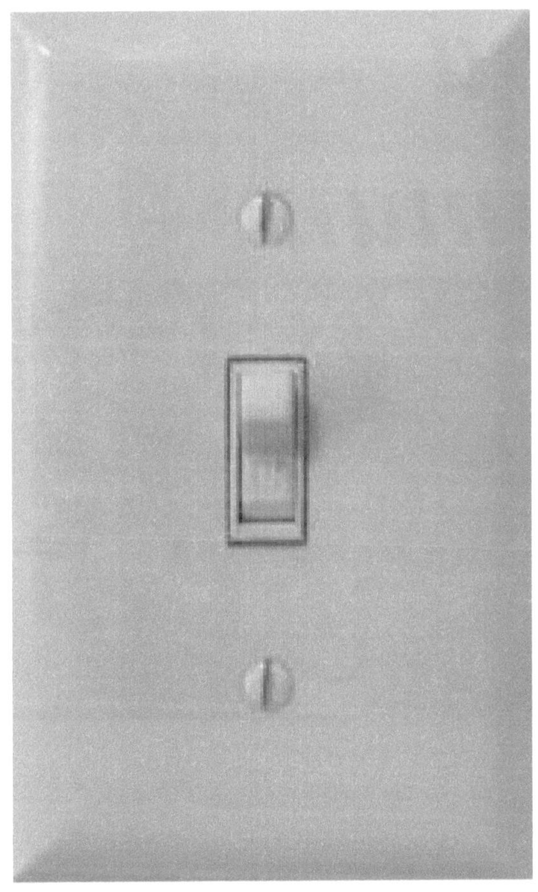

How to turn on a woman

It's so vitally important
that you
Satisfy one
another
To keep your
Love alive

Talk to each other, let
each other know what
you need, and find out
what they need.

You Have the Ability to Create Your Relationship Just the way You Want.

*Being
Selfish is
Not True
Love.
Let go and
Become
Selfless.*

Do you know
many couples
who split up only
to find the same
faults in their
next
relationship?
The only
difference is the
children suffer.

You're both good people.

Tomorrow is a new Day

Make it Work.

***Stuff's going to happen, Remember, talk it out! Don't Let it destroy your Marriage.**

If there's still a spark, a wish, a hope from each of you, then work it out or get help.

Find help from someone who will lead you down the path to love and Harmony

Fears, Hurts,
and Anger
will only
fester and
eventually be
the beginning
of the end for
you two.

Just let go and love!

Let's face it, Some couples just don't have the **desire** to make it work. But, That's Not YOU! Take the "high road", and make it work. One of you needs to stop the Nonsense! Be Brave! Speak up, tell them you want to make it work!

DECIDE
You are
determined
to <u>Really</u>
Make Your
**MARRIAGE
WORK.**

Now, Work it out and Let Go of...
Fears Hurts & Anger.

Be Brave

Put "All" Your
Heart out there
on your sleeve.
Yes, your heart
could be hurt,
Trust and
Be there for each
other.

Your Marriage is worth it

You've Got to want your Marriage to work, more than anything.

*Apologize
It can
change
everything*
You Know When
You Should,
Do it, even if You
Don't Want To.
Remember

*Trust the
INTENTION
of
Their Heart.*

Stop being Selfish, give without any expectation

*Focus on
What You
Love about
each other
&Appreciate
them.
Build each
other up*

Forgive

Let Go of Past Hurts

Tomorrow is a
New Day,
Forgive and
Forget.
Close the door on
the Past,
there is no way
you can change it
anyway.

Go
Forward
**Be Grateful
and
Love every
day
you have
together.**

"*Agree to Disagree*". *It's not Who's Right, It's What's Right.*

Men are the "fix it" species

When she's telling you what happened, you immediately go into Fixing it

"You don't need to be the Fix it man".

Just Listen!

Most of the time
that's all she
wants is for you to
just listen,
Really Listen.
If she wants your
help, or for you to
fix it, she'll ask
you what you
think, or she'll ask
for your help.

Show each other You are truly Interested *in what they have to* Say, *what they want to Do, what they want to Be.*

Everyone Loves to be heard and understood. Turn off the TV… No Interruption!

Realize, that Understanding one another is so Very Important.

What's going
on in their
mind and heart,
is really
Real for them.
Listen, so you
can be there for
them and
understand

Nagging
VS
Praising

Saying:
"You never
help me"
VS
"I Love it when
you help me"
Which do you
think is best?

Trust

And Be Trustworthy

Respect

Why do we have
a tendency to
treat strangers
nicer than we
treat each other.

*Give your all,
Even when
you don't
feel like it.*
This is Your
Marriage
Make it
work!

No one ever said
"marriage is
easy"
Right?
It takes 110% -
110%.
I know it's
impossible to
give 110% but
do it anyway.

*Support
Each Other
In Being the
Best person
they can Be*

Addictions and vices eventually cause damage. Put your foot down lovingly. There's no room for tolerance, it will only become worse. **Get help now.**

Cheating...
Don't

Cheating Will Change
Everything
Even if they
Never Find Out.
You will be different
&
Your relationship will
never be the same.

"A Family that Prays Together Stays Together"

Pray together.
Have Faith and
Trust in "God".
When you are stuck,
put it in "God's"
hands, then turn
toward one another
for love and support.

***Complaining
Is Repulsive.
It Repels Love.***

Complaining
Will Only Create
More to Complain
About Tomorrow.
Complaining will
become a habit.

Kids out of Control...

Kids can do a lot
of damage
to a marriage.
Take a parenting
class together.
Find a mentor or
teaching CD's or
online lessons.

Be Prepared

*Talk things over
with your
sweetheart, and
know how you will
respond to life's
challenges
And how, together,
you'll raise your
children.*

Children need You to be Consistent. They need to have balance, and know that when you say something you mean it and you will follow through.

Praise works well, everyone loves to be praised.

You are your children's example, they become little mirrors of you.
Join forces…
And Stay United in
Rearing Children.
Take control of Your home.

Make decisions
together, and
then
**Stick together
with your
decisions.**

Choose to Change, The Choice is Yours!

You've Got to want Your Marriage to work, More than the Air You Breathe.

Put your "ALL" into Your Relationship

Clean up,
smell good,
hair combed
and put on a
smile.
**Look your
best for
your
sweetie.**

Make a choice

Decide to

Be

In Love.

That means, You will Share Your Heart

Find Quality Time to be Together!

Even if it's just a little kiss or wink as you pass by one another.

Spending Quality Time is How You Ignite "Life" into your Marriage.

*Quality
Time
Is the
Greatest
Gift you can
Give each
other.*

*It is all up
to
YOU.*

Love with <u>ALL</u> Your Heart, and <u>M</u>iracles will come.